FRANCIS FRITH'S

HEADS OF THE VALLEYS

PHOTOGRAPHIC MEMORIES

ALAN GEORGE worked in Tredegar, whilst always residing in the Taff Valley. He has a special interest in photographs of the valleys and maintains an excellent website of old photos of Merthyr Tydfil with a colleague, Geoff Matsell. Originally from Pontypridd, **BEVERLEY ROBINS** is related to a Welsh rugby international and lives in a converted barn at Llwydcoed, Aberdare. She has worked with **CAROLYN JACOB**, the local studies librarian of Merthyr Tydfil, on several publishing projects, including a number of picture books and an annual heritage calendar.

FRANCIS FRITH'S
PHOTOGRAPHIC MEMORIES

HEADS OF THE VALLEYS

PHOTOGRAPHIC MEMORIES

ALAN GEORGE, CAROLYN JACOB
AND BEVERLEY ROBINS

First published in the United Kingdom in 2004 by
Frith Book Company Ltd

Limited Hardback Subscribers Edition Published in 2004
ISBN 1-85937-852-8

Paperback Edition 2004
ISBN 1-85937-853-6

British Library Cataloguing in Publication Data

Francis Frith's Heads of the Valleys - Photographic Memories
Alan George, Carolyn Jacob and Beverley Robins

Frith Book Company Ltd
Frith's Barn, Teffont,
Salisbury, Wiltshire SP3 5QP
Tel: +44 (0) 1722 716 376
Email: info@francisfrith.co.uk
www.francisfrith.co.uk

Printed and bound in Great Britain

Front Cover:
MERTHYR TYDFIL, *Upper High Street c1955* M118012t
Frontispiece:
ABERDARE, The *View from top of Craig c1960* A192002

*The colour-tinting is for illustrative purposes only, and is not intended
to be historically accurate*

CONTENTS

FRANCIS FRITH
VICTORIAN PIONEER

FRANCIS FRITH, founder of the world-famous photographic archive, was a complex and multi-talented man. A devout Quaker and a highly successful Victorian businessman, he was philosophical by nature and pioneering in outlook.

By 1855 he had already established a wholesale grocery business in Liverpool, and sold it for the astonishing sum of £200,000, which is the equivalent today of over £15,000,000. Now a very rich man, he was able to indulge his passion for travel. As a child he had pored over travel books written by early explorers, and his fancy and imagination had been stirred by family holidays to the sublime mountain regions of Wales and Scotland. 'What lands of spirit-stirring and enriching scenes and places!' he had written. He was to return to these scenes of grandeur in later years to 'recapture the thousands of vivid and tender memories', but with a different purpose. Now in his thirties, and captivated by the new science of photography, Frith set out on a series of pioneering journeys up the Nile and to the

Near East that occupied him from 1856 until 1860.

INTRIGUE AND EXPLORATION

These far-flung journeys were packed with intrigue and adventure. In his life story, written when he was sixty-three, Frith tells of being held captive by bandits, and of fighting 'an awful midnight battle to the very point of surrender with a deadly pack of hungry, wild dogs'. Wearing flowing Arab costume, Frith arrived at Akaba by camel sixty years before Lawrence of Arabia, where he encountered 'desert princes and rival sheikhs, blazing with jewel-hilted swords'.

He was the first photographer to venture beyond the sixth cataract of the Nile. Africa was still the mysterious 'Dark Continent', and Stanley and Livingstone's historic meeting was a decade into the future. The conditions for picture taking confound belief. He laboured for hours in his wicker dark-room in the sweltering heat of the desert, while the volatile chemicals fizzed dangerously in their trays. Back in London he exhibited his photographs and was 'rapturously cheered' by members of the Royal Society. His reputation as a photographer was made overnight.

VENTURE OF A LIFE-TIME

Characteristically, Frith quickly spotted the opportunity to create a new business as a specialist publisher of photographs. He lived in an era of immense and sometimes violent change.

For the poor in the early part of Victoria's reign work was exhausting and the hours long, and people had precious little free time to enjoy themselves. Most had no transport other than a cart or gig at their disposal, and rarely travelled far beyond the boundaries of their own town or village. However, by the 1870s the railways had threaded their way across the country, and Bank Holidays and half-day Saturdays had been made obligatory by Act of Parliament. All of a sudden the working man and his family were able to enjoy days out and see a little more of the world.

With typical business acumen, Francis Frith foresaw that these new tourists would enjoy having souvenirs to commemorate their days out. In 1860 he married Mary Ann Rosling and set out on a new career: his aim was to photograph every city, town and village in Britain. For the next thirty years he travelled the country by train and by pony and trap, producing fine photographs of seaside resorts and beauty spots that were keenly bought by millions of Victorians. These prints were painstakingly pasted into family albums and pored over during the dark nights of winter, rekindling precious memories of summer excursions.

THE RISE OF FRITH & CO

Frith's studio was soon supplying retail shops all over the country. To meet the demand he gathered about him a small team of photographers, and published the work of independent artist-photographers of the calibre of Roger Fenton and Francis Bedford. In order to gain some understanding of the scale of Frith's business one only has to look at the catalogue issued by Frith & Co in 1886: it runs to some 670 pages, listing not only many thousands of views of the British Isles but also many photographs of most European countries, and China, Japan, the USA and Canada - note the sample page shown on page 9 from the hand-written Frith & Co ledgers recording the pictures. By 1890 Frith had created the greatest specialist photographic publishing company in the world, with over 2,000 sales outlets - more than the combined number that Boots and WH Smith have today! The picture on the next page shows the Frith & Co display board at Ingleton in the Yorkshire Dales (left of window). Beautifully constructed with a mahogany frame and gilt inserts, it could display up to a dozen local scenes.

POSTCARD BONANZA

The ever-popular holiday postcard we know today took many years to develop. In 1870 the Post Office issued the first plain cards, with a pre-printed stamp on one face. In 1894 they allowed other publishers' cards to be sent through the mail with an attached adhesive halfpenny stamp. Demand grew rapidly, and in 1895 a new size of postcard was permitted called the court card, but there was little room for illustration. In 1899, a year after Frith's death, a new card measuring 5.5 x 3.5 inches became the standard format, but it was not until 1902 that the divided back came into being, so that the address and message could be on one face and a full-size illustration on the other. Frith & Co were in the vanguard of postcard development: Frith's sons Eustace and Cyril continued their father's monumental task, expanding the number of views offered to the public and recording more and more places in Britain, as the

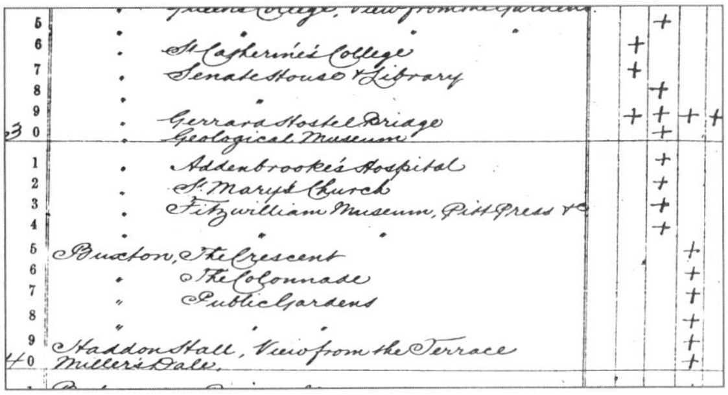

5	... College, View from the ...		+		
6	St Catherine's College	+			
7	Senate House & Library	+			
8			+		
9	Gerrard Hostel Bridge	+	+	+	+
30	Geological Museum		+		
1	Addenbrooke's Hospital		+		
2	St Mary's Church		+		
3	Fitzwilliam Museum, Pitt Press &c		+		
4			+		
5	Buxton, The Crescent			+	
6	The Colonnade			+	
7	Public Gardens			+	
8				+	
9	Haddon Hall, View from the Terrace			+	
40	Miller's Dale.			+	

coasts and countryside were opened up to mass travel.

Francis Frith had died in 1898 at his villa in Cannes, his great project still growing. The archive he created continued in business for another seventy years. By 1970 it contained over a third of a million pictures showing 7,000 British towns and villages.

FRANCIS FRITH'S LEGACY

Frith's legacy to us today is of immense significance and value, for the magnificent archive of evocative photographs he created provides a unique record of change in the cities, towns and villages throughout Britain over a century and more. Frith and his fellow studio photographers revisited locations many times down the years to update their views, compiling for us an enthralling and colourful pageant of British life and character.

We are fortunate that Frith was dedicated to recording the minutiae of everyday life. For it is this sheer wealth of visual data, the painstaking chronicle of changes in dress, transport, street layouts, buildings, housing, engineering and landscape that captivates us so much today. His remarkable images offer us a powerful link with the past and with the lives of our ancestors.

THE VALUE OF THE ARCHIVE TODAY

Computers have now made it possible for Frith's many thousands of images to be accessed almost instantly. Frith's images are increasingly used as visual resources, by social historians, by researchers into genealogy and ancestry, by architects and town planners, and by teachers involved in local history projects.

In addition, the archive offers every one of us an opportunity to examine the places where we and our families have lived and worked down the years. Highly successful in Frith's own era, the archive is now, a century and more on, entering a new phase of popularity. Historians consider the Francis Frith Collection to be of prime national importance. It is the only archive of its kind remaining in private ownership. Francis Frith's archive is now housed in an historic timber barn in the beautiful village of Teffont in Wiltshire. Its founder would not recognize the archive office as it is today. In place of the many thousands of dusty boxes containing glass plate negatives and an all-pervading odour of photographic chemicals, there are now ranks of computer screens. He would be amazed to watch his images travelling round the world at unimaginable speeds through internet lines.

The archive's future is both bright and exciting. Francis Frith, with his unshakeable belief in making photographs available to the greatest number of people, would undoubtedly approve of what is being done today with his lifetime's work. His photographs depicting our shared past are now bringing pleasure and enlightenment to millions around the world a century and more after his death.

HEADS OF
THE VALLEYS
AN INTRODUCTION

HOW GREEN were my valleys? Although there is an overwhelming industrial legacy in these towns, their rural heritage cannot be denied, and the beauty of the surrounding hills is now being lovingly restored. The various places illustrated in this book are neighbouring valleys, and they can collectively be described as 'The Heads of the Valleys'. The social development of the valleys is unique and fascinating.

Choral singing, politics, trade unions and rugby are all closely associated with the valleys, and account for much of the healthy inter-valley rivalry. However, they all have much more in common than they have aspects pulling them apart. These valleys all have similar characteristics, from dense terraced housing in a distinctive landscape, to chapel going and radical politics. Although some valleys are more anglicised than others, these are all working-class communities. They are made up of people who worked in common industries. The family historian will know that if an ancestor 'vanishes' from the Merthyr Tydfil census returns, he is likely to turn up on the census of Aberdare or Ebbw Vale. When work was in short supply in one valley, men would migrate to a more prosperous area.

The population mix of these valleys is diverse and interesting. The early industrial workers were an extraordinary mix from rural Wales, England and Ireland. Jewish, Spanish, and Italian migrants made their home here. If the Welsh were known for their coal, the Italians were renowned for their ice cream. At one point there were several hundred Italian cafes dotted throughout South Wales.

The leisure pursuits cherished in these communities were those that the people created themselves: chapels, churches, cinemas, and pubs. Music was important to the way of life. There were brass bands and jazz bands, but above all the people sang. Every chapel in every township had its choir, and periodically they would compete together in various competitions. The Aberdare United Choir, under the leadership of Caradoc, was the fruit of decades of effort by numerous enthusiasts. The literary and musical culture of all these valleys was outstanding, and there were rivalries between them when they competed at the Eisteddfod.

Chartism was common to all the valleys. Linked by politics, Aberdare and Merthyr Tydfil formed the same parliamentary constituency until after the First World War. South Wales is the stronghold of the Labour Party, and the Welsh miners and steelworkers have a tradition of independence of thought.

Possibly because of the importance of boxing and rugby here, these areas of heavy industry are wrongly thought of as outposts of male domination. However, Ieuan Gwynedd started the first magazine in Welsh for women in Tredegar, and, although the Jarrow March was a male-only affair, in the thirties many women accompanied the Aberdare and Merthyr Tydfil Hunger Marches to London. None can deny the vital role of the Welsh 'mam' here.

Rivers play a crucial part in these valleys. Aberdare, Ebbw Vale and Merthyr Tydfil are the most important towns in their respective river valleys. The topography comprising this area is diverse, as it consists of steep sides, flattened river bottoms, sparsely grassed plateaux and rocky outcrops. Aberdare, set in attractive scenery at the head of the Cynon Valley, is at the confluence of the Dare stream with the river Cynon. Ebbw Vale is in the valley of the river Ebbw, and Brynmawr in that of the Ebbw Fach. The river Taff runs through the parish of Merthyr Tydfil. The name of the Rhymney river is derived from the Welsh word for 'augur', something that bores through the land, and the river was formerly the boundary between Glamorgan and Monmouthshire. The river Sirhowy rises north of Tredegar at the quarrying village of Trefil, and must be one of the fastest flowing rivers in Britain. Once blackened and polluted by industry, the rivers in these valleys today have sparkling waters which contain trout once again.

The valleys of Wales have plentiful rainfall and produce a large surplus of water, which,

owing to the physical features of the valleys, is comparatively easy and cheap to harness and exploit. The landscape here defies attempts to view it from a single perspective. The travel writers of the 19th century delighted in the beautiful scenery of this area, when oak covered much of the region and the rest was green agricultural land. There are still remnants of a more rural age dotted through the valleys: some traditional old Welsh long houses, old farms and even ruined castles, which are to be found here as everywhere in Wales.

Although this area has unquestionably been ravaged by heavy industry, the scars of the former industrial period were beginning to heal by the 1960s, as clean modern factories sprang up on the sites of the old iron and steel works. However, there are industrial remains here. Some of the buildings of the ironmasters can still be seen, including the magnificent Tredegar House, home of the Homfrays, and the splendid Cyfarthfa Castle, belonging to the Crawshays. Three arches remain of the Sirhowy ironworks, and in Rhymney is Butetown, the model workers' village with a symmetrical layout. The original tramway used by Richard Trevithick 200 years ago is being restored. At Robertstown, Aberdare, there is a cast iron tram bridge, which carried horse-drawn trams across the river from 1811 onwards. There has been a deliberate attempt to clean up and remove any dangerous remains of industry. Recent landscaping, restoration and regeneration have altered the look of the valleys. Today, near the Heads of the Valleys Road, industrial remains stand alongside peacefully grazing sheep.

Merthyr Tydfil lies at the head of the Taff Valley. The history of this area can be neatly summed up by four words: castles, coal, chapels and Crawshays. The Crawshay family was prominent in many of the valleys. Merthyr Tydfil, with an ancient medieval castle, was the first small settlement to change and grow with industrialisation. The Crawshays created a castle as their private residence and fled from it during the Merthyr Rising of 1831. Immigrants poured into these valleys, and there was a time when Merthyr Tydfil was the fastest growing town in the world and the only large town in Wales. The name Merthyr means 'burial place of a saint'. The parish church is dedicated to Saint Tydfil, reputed to have been a martyred Christian princess. The town may have been at the cutting edge of the Industrial Revolution and 'the iron capital of the world', but it is set in beautiful rural countryside at the foothills of the Brecon Beacons.

At the head of the Cynon Valley, Aberdare, 'Queen of the Valleys', and famed for steam coal, was still a busy mining town when the photographs in this book were taken. In recent years the old heavy industries have been replaced, but nearby is the only remaining Welsh deep mine, Tower Colliery. Aberdare is the only British town to have a bronze statue of a musician conducting a choir as its main monument. It represents Caradog, who led the South Wales Choral Union to victory in the competitions at the Crystal Palace in 1872 and 1873.

Rhymney is situated on the border of the three counties of Breconshire, Glamorgan and Monmouthshire. There is a romantic legend connected with the area: the 'eyes of Rhymney', two springs, are said to weep when things go wrong in the valley.

The eastern heads of their respective valleys, Brynmawr, Ebbw Vale and Tredegar, were all the products of the early days of the Industrial Revolution, and important industrial centres in their own right. Tredegar, named after the seat of Lord Tredegar, has an open mountain plateau and exhilarating air. There is a strong tradition of political activity here. Tredegar was the home of Aneurin Bevan, and Michael Foot was the MP for Ebbw Vale. Ebbw Vale had the largest tinplate strip mill in Britain, as well as a thriving coal mining industry. Brynmawr was at one time the largest town in the rural county of Breconshire, but the county boundaries have all altered, and it is not in present day Powys but in Gwent. During the industrial depression of the 1930s, Brynmawr was greatly affected. A rubber factory was built to provide local jobs for a disadvantaged community; it was an impressive post-war modernist concrete building with a vast and spectacular vaulted column-free production area. Unfortunately, this idiosyncratic building has now been dismantled.

These communities all witnessed many changes because of increased industrialisation. The industries changed from 'Welsh' iron-puddling (the Welsh developed a superior method of iron-puddling often referred to as the Welsh method) to huge steel blast furnaces, and from small coal patches and levels to great deep coal pits employing over 2,000 men. The people in these communities of deep and narrow valleys were frequently referred to in Government reports as 'people from the Hill Districts'. These valleys of great natural beauty were savagely exploited by industry, and the landscape is pock-marked and damaged by man. This area produced the steam coal that powered the British Navy and created huge wealth for some, but in the thirties its industrial base was completely eroded. Coal mines and steel plants closed down, and there was great unemployment. The valleys were united by the bonds of deprivation and poverty. For a hundred years migrant workers were drawn here for employment, but during the thirties there was a huge migration from the valleys to the Midlands and London. After the Second World War the valleys underwent a re-birth and regeneration, as new industries were brought in to diversify industry here. The valley bottoms now house a new generation of retail parks, set alongside car parks for their employees. Photographs in this book show some of the modern post-war buildings, which were fashionably new when the pictures were taken.

In practical terms, what links the towns in this book is the Heads of the Valleys Road, the A465, which runs from Abergavenny to Neath. Throughout the 19th century, access in South Wales meant little more than providing the means of moving coal, limestone, iron and steel. The valleys all grew as independent units, and links between them were underdeveloped. It was ridiculous, but journeys between one valley and another had to be made via Newport or Cardiff. A government programme of road improvement to correct this situation was started in the 1960s, and the Heads of the Valleys Road is the result. Today, sections of the most dangerous stretches of the road are in the process of been widened. The view from the Heads of the Valleys road has changed considerably in the last thirty years.

The history of South Wales is unquestionably linked to the iron and coal industries. Early industrial developments in Wales took place high up the valleys, even within the attractive area now designated the Brecon Beacons National Park. The old image of black tips and derelict mines is a far cry from the present reality. The woodlands, consisting of oak, silver birch, beech and hawthorn, now contain a variety of habitats for bird life, and the mighty red kite has now ventured beyond mid Wales to the Heads of the Valleys.

The area faces the future with growing confidence. The shops in the various town centres have altered since the pictures in this book were taken, and many town centres have now been pedestrianised. There are still street markets in many towns. Renewal and regeneration has not been easy, nor is it complete, but the Garden Festival of Wales site at Ebbw Vale shows what can be done, and some areas have improved beyond all recognition. The valleys are not what they were: they can no longer be characterised as rows of long dreary terraces of cottages. Miners exercising their whippets on the mountainsides are firmly a thing of the past. Today, wooded hills and beautiful rivers make the scenery attractive again. However, the past must not be forgotten. The history of the area is the history of small people, who made ironmasters and coal owners rich, but who also fought hard for their rights and survived, together with the towns they created, much longer than the industry that brought them here.

HEADS OF
THE VALLEYS

ABERAMAN, *Lewis Street c1955* A189001

There is a substantial garage here with two pumps (right), although at this time there were usually only one or two car owners in each street, and not surprisingly few cars are shown. A café and tobacconist are situated next to the impressive-looking chapel. There was a Co-op branch in this street, and Mainwaring's (extreme left) was an important store here.

◄**ABERAMAN**
Victoria Place c1955
A189002

This town developed around the ironworks, which were founded by Crawshay Bailey in 1846. The population of six thousand at the beginning of the 20th century had all the variety of shops necessary for a thriving independent community. Today there is an open space where once stood the impressive Public Hall and Institute (right).

◄**ABERDARE**
General View 1937
87886

We are looking down on Aberdare, a town set amid beautiful scenery at the head of the Cynon Valley. On the far right, the road continues over the top to Maerdy. In this area there are a number of the many valley roads built during the depression of the 1920s and 1930s by the unemployed under the Public Works scheme.

◄**ABERAMAN**
St Margaret's Church c1955 A189007

This Anglican church was built at a cost of £3,000 in the early 1860s. Sir George Elliott, who funded most of the cost, held a sumptuous banquet to mark its opening. Its attractive Victorian design provided plenty of room for the growing congregation of a developing town.

ABERDARE, *St Elvan's Church 1937* 87887

The 'Cathedral of the Valleys', St Elvan's is an elegant Anglican church constructed of Bath stone and commanding a hillside position. It was intended to set architectural standards in the rapidly growing industrial town. Finance came from numerous sources, including the Abernant Iron Company and J Bruce Pryce of Duffryn. When St Elvan's was opened for public worship in September 1852 it was described as 'an ornament of ecclesiastical art not to be equalled in the Principality'. It is uncertain as to whether Elvan was a Roman or a Briton, but he is credited with helping to convert Britain to Christianity.

▲ ABERDARE, *The Park 1937* 87888

The public park in Aberdare was opened amid the firing of cannons in July 1869. The spaciousness of the Cynon Valley is proudly exhibited in this splendid park flanking the Aberdare town centre. The photograph was taken in an era in which all men wore a hat denoting their employment status; the gentleman with the stick and bowler hat is probably an important civic officer.

◄ *detail from 87888*

▲ **ABERDARE**
   The Park and the Lake 1937 87889

This picture was taken during a time of
high unemployment in Aberdare, and the
scene shows men at leisure. Boating was a
popular pastime with all social classes.
Mr Isaac Thomas obtained permission to
place three pleasure boats on the Lake in
May 1887, but he had to provide a
suitable landing stage and a lodge for the
person in charge.

▶ *detail from 87889*

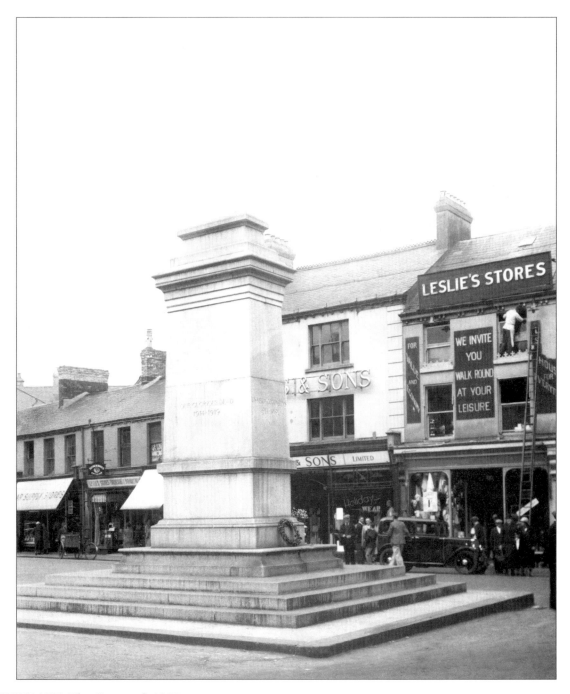

ABERDARE, *The Cenotaph 1937* 87890

The Aberdare memorial to the First World War has an unusual cenotaph design similar to the one in London. The premises of Haydn W Morris, an optician, are on the left-hand side of the photograph. Leslie's (right) was a popular store; it had a special toy fair each October, and a Father Christmas from November onwards.

▶ **ABERDARE**
*The View from
the Top of Craig
c1960* A192002

Looking east towards
Merthyr Tydfil, this
photograph shows
the spaciousness of
this broad wide-open
valley, nicknamed the
'Queen of the Valleys'.
In the foreground are
rows of turn of the
century terraces. The
spire of St Elvan's
dominates the
landscape.

◀**ABERDARE**
*The Park Entrance and
the Boys' County
School 1937*
87891

The area on the right,
opposite the lower entrance
to the park, was known as
'Commin Bach'. When the
school was opened in 1896
the original building did not
have a clock tower - this was
added later. The statue of W
T Lewis, Lord Merthyr (left),
is identical to a statue which
stood beside the General
Hospital in Merthyr Tydfil.

▲ **ABERDARE**, *Monk Street and St Elvan's Church c1955* A192004

This quiet residential street reflects an age without many cars. On the top of the street is the turning to the Aberdare County Park, and the road is going up to Maerdy in the Rhondda. As we looking down Monk Street, we can see the elegant spire of St Elvan's Church at the bottom of the street.

◄ **ABERDARE**
The County School for Boys c1955 A192006

Aberdare was chosen as the venue for one of the Intermediate schools in Glamorgan. The memorial stone was laid on 10 August 1893 by Lord Aberdare. The new school opened in 1896 with room for 100 boys and 80 girls, with a catchment area extending from Rhigos to Mountain Ash.

ABERDARE, *The Caradog Memorial c1955* A192011

The bronze statue shows Griffith Rhys Jones (Caradog) conducting the South Wales Choral Union to victory at Crystal Palace in 1872 and 1873. This impressive work by Goscombe John cost £1,500, raised by public subscription, and it was unveiled by Lord Aberdare on 10 July 1920. Here Caradog is in his original place; in 1962 he was moved to a position beside the Black Lion Hotel.

ABERDARE
Cardiff Street c1955
A192013

The clock on the front of the Aberdare and District Co-operative Society (right) dates from the thirties, when the building was rebuilt. The Co-op dominated this street: drapery and millinery were at number 9 Cardiff Street, and the main part with food, ironmongery, and footwear was at numbers 3, 4 and 5. This elegant building was improved in 1965, but the store finally closed in 1988.

ABERDARE, *Cannon Street c1955* A192016

In this wide street, cars can park on both sides of the road and still allow for traffic. Cannon Street is one of the oldest parts of the town, and dates from the 1850s. The river Dare runs underneath this main shopping street. The Queen's Hotel, which later became Burton's (right), stood in Cannon Street.

ABERDARE
Commercial Street
c1955 A192018

There was once a railway crossing at the bottom of Commercial Street, the main business centre of the town. At the time of this photograph Aberdare was beginning to revive its fortunes following the depression and the Second World War. New factories, such as Cable, were set up from the 1930s.

ABERDARE
The Square c1955
A192019

The popular Café Mona with its triangular roof stands out at the back of the picture. Aberdare still has the feel of a pleasant market town about it. This scene would have been very similar 20 years previously, but today it has changed dramatically, although Barclays Bank is still on the corner.

◄ ABERDARE
Ystradfellte Falls c1955
A192039

Situated in the Brecon Beacons National Park, these splendid waterfalls are still a major tourist attraction in the area, although they are associated with a number of tragedies. Even in recent years these deep pools have been associated with tragic drowning incidents concerning children and despite their natural beauty they have to be approached with care. The isolated community of Ystradfellte only has an ancient church, a pub, and a few houses, but it is surrounded by some of the most magnificent limestone scenery in Wales.

◄ **ABERDARE**
The Hospital c1955
A192031

In the early seventies the attractive gardens around this hospital were greatly reduced in order to create a new maternity block for the hospital. This small hospital has been under threat of closure, but in 2004 it is still battling to keep open.

◄ **ABERDARE**
Cardiff Street c1955 A192053

There appears to be only one car on the road; however, in the left-hand corner there is a wheeled vehicle on the pavement. Many shops have changed today, and the Aberdare Furnishing Company store (third from the left) is now B Wise. In this street there was a wonderful Italian café, Servini; originally selling cigarettes and drinks, it gradually extended to become a smart restaurant, as well as a café open all hours. Servini was popular. The food was excellent, and the atmosphere was very friendly and informal, as was the town of Aberdare as a whole.

▶ **ABERDARE**
Victoria Square
c1960 A192076

Victoria Square was originally called Commercial Place, and hackney cabs operated from stands here. The flower gardens have been replaced by a one-way system. The Castle Hotel once stood on the left-hand side, but today there is a National Westminster Bank on this corner. The Bute Arms (further down the street on the left) gets its name from the Marquises of Bute, great landowners in South Wales and important nationally.

◀ **ABERDARE**
The Boot Hotel
c1960 A192079

The Boot Hotel is an old coaching inn with a central position. To its left was Café Mona, the place to go for special occasions. The silver service waitresses, in black and white uniforms, served wonderful cakes from elegant high cake stands.

▲ **ABERDARE,** *St John's Church c1965* A192107

The old parish church of St John was built of local materials to a simple design. The church was originally built before 1200, making it a link with the pre-industrial past. The victims of the dreadful cholera epidemic of 1849 were buried here. Today, St John's Church stands in an 'open plan' churchyard surrounded by modern buildings, such as the Library.

◀**ABERDARE**
The Black Lion c1965
A192110

This is Victoria Street, with the Caradoc statue in the centre of the photograph. The Black Lion (centre left) was originally a Victorian public house, and in the fifties it was commonly used for wedding receptions and private parties. Today the pub goes by the shortened name of simply the Black, and the word 'Lion' has been painted over. There was once a commemorative Queen Victoria water trough in Victoria Square, but it has disappeared.

ABERDARE
Cannon Street
A192113

This scene recalls the time when there were far fewer cars and two-way traffic ran along Cannon Street. There are a good variety of shops here, Morris (second from the right, selling ladies' clothing), Snooks the gents' hairdresser next door, and so on. Originally the lands upon which Cannon Street and the streets to the north now stand (called Maesydre) were considered to be only fit for the keeping of horses.

BRYNMAWR, *Beaufort Street c1950* B730003

The most surprising feature of this busy shopping scene is the complete lack of any vehicles. Typically there is a group of young women on the left-hand side more interested in having a chat than in shopping, but two ladies look eagerly into the windows of F C Cable opposite. At the bottom of the street on the left stands the New Griffin Hotel, an important landmark in this street.

▲ BRYNMAWR
Alma Street c1950 B730012

This is the entrance to Brynmawr from Abergavenny. There are impressive old cars in this residential street, including an Armstrong-Siddeley and a Wolseley. The classic street lamp (left) is alongside number 46, and Trafalgar House was one of the large expensive houses on the other side of the road.

◀ *detail from B730012*

▼ **BRYNMAWR,** *Alma Street and King Street c1950* B730013

The Heads of the Valleys Road had not been built when this picture was taken, as it shows the A465 old Merthyr road leading into King Street, Brynmawr. The road on the left is the old tram road used in the time of Crawshay Bailey. The photograph does not quite capture the Bridge End Inn on the extreme right.

▶ **BRYNMAWR**
Clydach from the Hafod Road c1955
B730031

This photograph shows Llanelly Hill and the old lime kilns. The road on the right had an extremely steep gradient and was the old roadway before the Heads of the Valleys Road. Alongside it was the house belonging to the manager of the ironworks.

◀ **BRYNMAWR**
Beaufort Street
c1955 B730048

The Griffin Bus Company, which was later taken over by Red and White in 1947, had a base in Brynmawr. Eastmans the butcher's (right) has a young customer waiting outside. It is interesting to note that the nearby pedestrian is carefully avoiding walking under the ladder.

▶ **BRYNMAWR**
The Square c1955
B730049

The First World War memorial has a central position here. This picture was taken before the building of the bus station. The Griffin bus went to Blackwood at 5 minutes past each hour, and Ralphs bus journeyed to Newport at a quarter past the hour.

BRYNMAWR
The Swimming Pool
c1955 B730052

Outdoor swimming pools were a feature of the concern for health and fitness in the 1930s. The Brynmawr pool was built with help from the Quakers, and Lord Haw Haw, the Second World War traitor (his real name was William Joyce), worked on the project when he was a student. This must have been a hot day, as a number of children are sun bathing, but it is hard to imagine the temperature of the water here as anything but freezing. The diving board here was known locally as the 'plachet', and as you became a better swimmer you moved upwards to a higher level.

► **BRYNMAWR**
Beaufort Street
c1955 B730054

Despite one motor
car, which is possibly
a Ford 8, the shoppers
here feel safe enough
to saunter slowly up
the road ignoring the
pavement. On the
left-hand side was
W J Price, a chemist's,
and the New Griffin
pub, and on the right
were the Wine Vaults
and Betty's ladies'
and children's wear.

◄ **BRYNMAWR**
The Market Square
1955 B730071

The original Market Hall
clock was presented by
Mr Charles Morley. The
Market Hall itself has
undergone many
architectural changes
throughout the 20th
century, and today the
charming Market Hall
Cinema is one of the few
publicly owned cinemas
in the country. The post-
war Red and White bus is
probably the five past
two going to Crickhowell
on a Sunday afternoon.

▲ **BRYNMAWR,** *From Blaenavon Road c1960* B730084

Here we see Brynmawr, the highest town in South Wales, from the old Blaenavon Road; this is one part of Brynmawr which has not changed at all. Sheep feeding on the fringes of a valley town are still a common sight. Agriculture and heavy industry always existed side by side, and coal miners grew their own vegetables and kept hens and pigs.

◄ **BRYNMAWR**
The Heads of the Valleys Road c1960
B730097

The coming of the Heads of the Valleys Road greatly changed the landscape of this area. Today this busy road is rarely as quiet as this. It has a reputation as one of the most dangerous roads in Britain, and it is in the process of being improved and widened to make it safer.

BRYNMAWR
The Bus Station c1965
B730100

This must have been the most exposed, wind-swept bus station in Wales. Brynmawr was once the largest town in the rural county of Breconshire, but in 1974 it became part of industrial Gwent. The Red and White bus is probably a Bristol make. The Roman Catholic church and school is behind the bus station.

43

▶ **BRYNMAWR**
The Semtex Factory
c1965 B730103

After much lobbying, notably by the leading Quaker, Lord Jim Forrester, the Dunlop Semtex factory was constructed between 1948 and 1950. The factory considerably alleviated the serious unemployment problem in the area, and produced a variety of rubber goods. Its innovative concrete design with its vast and spectacular vaulted column-free production area (its design was apparently based on the Festival Hall in London) led to its being declared a listed building after its closure in 1981. Unfortunately, it has been demolished, despite protests.

◀ **BRYNMAWR**
Beaufort Street c1965
B730105

Surely this quiet scene looking up Beaufort Street was taken on a Sunday morning, for otherwise there would be some shoppers in this busy commercial street. The two shops below the sign for Clarks' shoes (right) were Briggs Shoes and Briggs Baby Wear.

◄ **BRYNMAWR**
The Church c1965
B730117

The parish church of Brynmawr is the church of St Mary the Virgin, and it was opened by the licence of the Bishop of St David's in January 1850. It is of a functional, practical design, and its founding was recognition that the town of Brynmawr was an independent community.

45

EBBW VALE
Bethcar Street c1950
E176007

The Bon Marche on Bethcar Street was a large general department store, selling practically anything. By the time this picture was taken, it had become the recently renovated indoor market. The White House Cinema is situated near the Midland Bank. The Red and White bus disappearing in the distance was specially built for the area: it was one of the first double-decker buses for low bridges.

◄ EBBW VALE
The Arches c1955
E176010

The area is known locally as the Crescent. This stone arch was built in 1869 to carry raw materials to the iron furnaces. A pedestrian tunnel was added beside the main arch owing to the increase in traffic. At the top of the steps on the right was a fish and chip shop; its practice of throwing out vinegar caused the area to be nicknamed Vinegar Hill.

◄**EBBW VALE**
Newtown c1955 E176012

The first part of Newtown was built as workers' cottages for
the employees of the ironworks, and the other section was
for workers in the brick works. These early industrial
houses no longer remain, but the Britannia Inn, where the
workers drank, has survived from the 1840s. The Bridge
End public house (right) has much more recent origins.

▼ **EBBW VALE**
Bethcar Street c1955 E176014

At this time, few people went even as far as Newport to
shop, and shopping locally was an opportunity to gossip
with friends. This street has undergone a number of
recent changes, and is now fully pedestrianised. Bethcar
chapel has become the Public Library

EBBW VALE
The Roundabout c1955
E176018

We are looking north from the roundabout, and the Catholic church is just visible in the distance at the end of James Street. The railway lines and signal indicate that the LMS High Level Station is still in use, although the railway line and station soon disappeared owing to the closures of the 1960s and the redevelopment of the town centre. The railway line crossing the main road was the mineral line to Trevil Quarry. The roundabout was essential to enable the buses to turn round here.

◄ **EBBW VALE**
*The Old Age
Pensioners' Hall
c1960* E176028

The building of this hall reflected the growing prosperity of the Ebbw Vale, which was due to almost full employment after 1938. For a time the local Operatic Society made use of the hall. This scene, showing the council canteen and Eureka Place at the top left, has greatly changed, and there is now a shopping centre nearby.

◄ **EBBW VALE**
The Welfare Ground
c1955 E176025

Built on the site of old levels, this playing field represented a pleasant green area in the midst of heavy industry. The old caretaker's house has now been replaced by an indoor sports pavilion. The Welfare Ground's two stands and a floodlight system were erected in the late 1950s. The terracing in the picture has now been replaced.

◄ **EBBW VALE**
The Gorsedd Stones
c1960 E176035

The stones for the Gorsedd Circle were quarried at the Trefil Quarry. They were later removed to their present site when the park was altered to make room for an extension to the steel works. Today the Gorsedd Circle Stones, first erected for the 1958 National Eisteddfod, can be found in a sunken garden to the north of the town centre near the River Ebbw.

EBBW VALE
General View c1955
E176036

The elegant 75-foot spire of Christ Church is prominent in the landscape; the old ironworks and spoil tips are behind it. The terraces of Newtown are to the right. The railway network serviced the iron and steel furnaces, and the railway wagons were unloaded directly into the furnaces. Penuel chapel is in the centre, and to its left is Wilputte Terrace, named after a Belgian gentleman.

EBBW VALE, *Christ Church c1960* E176043

This church was built on a steep hillside between 1859 and 1861, but the tower and spire were added between 1884 and 1886. The architect was the popular John Norton of Bristol. The building was expensive, and the final cost of the church was thought to be nearly £60,000. The first service took place here in December 1861 - and yet the consecration of the church by the Bishop of Llandaff was not until August 1869.

EBBW VALE
Bethcar Street c1960
E176056

On the right in this busy scene can be seen the original Co-operative store and the old police station. Ida Place, named after the wife of Jonathan Davies, who built the street, is to the left; the popular Queen's Café stands next to Johnson's the cleaner's. Bethcar was a 'respectable' street, unlike Victoria Road, which was known as 'Gin-shop hill'.

EBBW VALE, *The Black Mountains c1960* E176064

The Black Mountains, although challenging for walkers, are less barren than the Brecon Beacons. The tranquillity of the rounded hills were once often in stark contrast to the heavy industry below. This view shows the old road from the Heads of the Valleys to Ebbw Vale and Blaenavon.

► **EBBW VALE**
From Beaufort Hill
c1960 E176069

Ebbw Vale did not begin to take shape until the 1860s. Before this date there were three separate industrial settlements, Beaufort in the north, Ebbw Vale in the centre, and Victoria in the south. Each community was distinct, with its own sense of identity. The air here, once so dense with the smoke of the ironworks, is now crisp and clear.

◄ EBBW VALE
Mountain Ponies c1960
E176074

The ponies are grazing on Waun y Pound Common; Ebbw Vale College is behind them and Newtown is in the background. Horses were once the backbone of coal mining in South Wales, but today they are no longer used in industry. The hills too have changed, as slag tips have been removed and are now green slopes.

▶ **EBBW VALE**
The Old Arch
c1960 E176079

This is one of the significant relics of the industrial past of the Ebbw Vale area, and at one time a busy railway line ran over the top of this arch. There are two dates on the keystone: the bridge of 1867 collapsed and was replaced by another in 1869.

▶ **EBBW VALE**
The Steelworks c1960 E176080

Ebbw Vale was one of the first steelworks. Bessemer steel was produced here as early as 1866, and this process continued until the last Bessemer blow in 1962. The Bessemer industrial process of rendering cast iron malleable by the introduction of air into the fluid metal to remove carbon was an improved iron smelting process that produced large quantities of ingots of superior quality. (Modern steel is made using technology based on Bessemer's process) This photograph was taken as the Bessemer era was finally coming to an end. After a successful history of making iron, the furnaces ceased production in 1974.

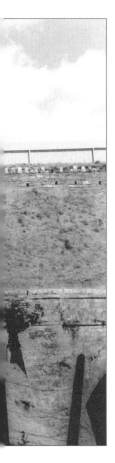

▲ **HIRWAUN,** *The Cenotaph, High Street c1960* H291004

Behind the solid First World War Memorial is the Cardiff Arms, a public house often used for wedding reception that is still a popular watering hole today. At one time there was certainly no drinking after hours here because both the landlady's daughters were policewomen.

▲ **HIRWAUN** *c1955* H291002

From the elevated position of the bowling green there is a panoramic view overlooking Hirwaun, encompassing rural scenery and industry. Beside the distant railway station, the chimney of the old brickworks stands out on the skyline. The background has changed dramatically but the bowling green is still used by local and visiting bowlers.

▶ **MERTHYR TYDFIL**
High Street c1906
M118001

Many aspects of the
social history of the
town are captured in
this photograph. The
horse-drawn vehicles,
which include a bus,
reflect more primitive
modes of transport.
There was an electric
tram system established
at this time, but it did
not extend as far as the
lower High Street.

◄ **MERTHYR TYDFIL**
High Street c1955 M118002

These businesses opposite the library and St David's Church have changed since this picture was taken. Today the Castle cinema is closed, and the Electric cinema (right) has now gone. The Peter Pan Café (left), once famous for holding wedding receptions, Hodges & Sons (next door but one, selling menswear), J Baker & Sons (a shoe shop) and Olivers - all these have gone. The prestigious department store, Manchester House (centre), has changed hands several times; it was converted into a public house in the Weatherspoons chain in the 1990s. The National Savings Centre (second from left) was established during the Second World War, and at this time sold 6d stamps with a picture of Princess Anne

▼ **MERTHYR TYDFIL**
Pontmorlais Circus c1955 M118005

Pontmorlais was once a thriving commercial centre. Flook's the jeweller's (the third awning from the left), founded in the 19th century, is still trading today. However, a number of the buildings here have been demolished, including the Palace Cinema, the Owen Glyndwr and the Park Café (next door but one to Flook's). The Palace Cinema had a number of shows each day in the 1950s, and the programme changed twice a week. Once you paid for a ticket you could stay all day. There was bingo every Tuesday and Thursday in the Palace Ballroom, later the Sands Dance Hall. A policeman controls the non-existent traffic, but waits with anticipation for the approach of another vehicle.

▼ **MERTHYR TYDFIL,** *The Recreation Ground c1955* M118008

Three tennis courts and a bowling green were added to the Thomastown Park in the inter-war years. This amenity, known locally as the 'old park', was built on the waste tips of the Penydarren Ironworks. The park is within easy access of the town, and so full use was always made of the amenities provided.

► **MERTHYR TYDFIL**
Upper High Street
c1955 M118012

Three public houses in the photograph are still in business: the Express, the Anchor Inn and the Vulcan are virtually unchanged. Shatz & Sons (fourth from the right) was a furnishing business established in 1891, with a wholesale warehouse in the High Street and a showroom in Post Office Lane. Humphreys hardware shop next door spanned a hundred years before it ceased trading.

◄ **MERTHYR TYDFIL**
Cyfarthfa Castle Museum c1955
M118016

Cyfarthfa Castle was built in 1825 for the Crawshay family, the ironmasters; then it was bought by the Merthyr Tydfil Corporation in 1909 for £19,700. Part of the ground floor was opened as a municipal museum and art gallery in 1910, and the remaining section became a secondary school in 1912. This is still the situation today.

▶ **MERTHYR TYDFIL**
Cyfarthfa Park c1955 M118021

New roads and paths were constructed when this private garden became a public park. The park is well timbered with established trees that have taken a lifetime to grow. There are lawns and flower-beds, rock gardens, extensive shrubberies, and miles of woodland walks.

▶ **MERTHYR TYDFIL**
Pontsarn c1955
M118025

Pontsarn has a peaceful rural location. Dowlais was its nearest town, and the industrial workers always enjoyed the beautiful scenery here. The houses on the left are extremely old. The Monkey Puzzle tree is a symbol of good luck and a sign of wealth.

◄ **MERTHYR TYDFIL**
Pontsarn Viaduct c1960
M118026

This viaduct was constructed to carry the Brecon and Merthyr Railway over the Taff Fechan River. Like the Cefn Coed Viaduct, it was designed and built by Savin and Ward and their chief engineer, Alexander Sutherland. It is a Grade II listed structure, but the parapet is decaying, several stones have become dislodged, and various shrubs and trees are growing in the masonry jointing.

▼ **MERTHYR TYDFIL,** *The Pontsarn Hotel c1960* M118027

This was still a popular venue for summer trips and Sunday School outings in the sixties. Following the railway journey, which was frequently a short one, the day-trippers could find suitable refreshments in the Pontsarn Hotel. There are 99 steps from the Pontsarn Hotel down to the Blue Pool.

▶ **MERTHYR TYDFIL**
The Blue Pool c1960
M118030

So called because of the darkness of its waters, the Blue Pool is formed by the Taff Fechan. It has delighted many generations of youngsters, who have enjoyed bathing here on hot summer days. The common practice was for lads to push each other in before hauling each other out.

◀ **MERTHYR TYDFIL**
Gellideg Estate
c1955 M118031

Constructed for Merthyr Council, the modern houses in this estate were built in this high and somewhat exposed position to replace some of the worst housing in the Borough. Gellideg is the name of one of the ancient hamlets of the parish. This shows the first or 'lower' entrance; the sign of the builders, Dickinson, is still visible (bottom, centre right). The majority of these houses are semi-detached with very large rear gardens.
To halt the decline of the Gellideg Estate, in recent years it has been part of a Community Regeneration Programme.

▶ **MERTHYR TYDFIL**
General View
c1960 M118033

This photograph was taken from the former tip on the Swansea Road. The corner of the Gellideg chapel is on the far left, and the old Gellideg houses are in the centre. The Swansea Road is on the right-hand side, together with a short cut to Heolgerrig. The Thorn Electric Factory, which was built on the site of the Cyfarthfa works, is clearly visible.

MERTHYR TYDFIL
The Public Library
c1960 M118035

This scene is quite similar today. The old Town Hall to the left of the library is rather more dilapidated, but it has survived being struck by lightning. There are still benches beside Lord Buckland's statue (left), but the events notice board has been removed. The library always opens all its windows in hot weather.

MERTHYR TYDFIL, *Thomastown Park c1960* M118036

In 1900 Thomastown Park, built on the site of an old quarry, was the first public park in the Borough. Situated east of the town, the total area of the park covers 17 acres. This part is known locally as 'the new park', and it is secluded and peaceful.

MERTHYR TYDFIL
The Flower Gardens, Cyfarthfa Castle c1955 M118040

Following the purchase of Cyfarthfa Castle for the town in 1909, the grounds became a public park; it was a source of great pleasure to Keir Hardie, the MP for Merthyr, that he was able to open up the 160 acres of a former grand private garden to the ordinary citizens of the town.

MERTHYR TYDFIL, *Cyfarthfa Castle c1955* M118041

An interesting side view of Cyfarthfa Castle. This grand regency mansion was designed by Robert Lugar, an architect who specialised in castellated buildings. The Castle has 365 windows, one for every day of the year and originally had a total of 72 rooms. It overlooked the Cyfarthfa Ironworks and the remains of these furnaces may still be seen.

▼ **MERTHYR TYDFIL,** *The Lake, Cyfarthfa Castle c1960* M118044

The lake in Cyfarthfa Park covers nearly 7 acres. It was used for boating in pre-Second World War days, but after this it slowly ceased to be used for this purpose. A former boat house was demolished before this picture was taken. The lake is still open to the public for fishing.

► **MERTHYR TYDFIL**
Morlais Castle c1960
M118052

Merthyr Tydfil still has the ruins of a medieval castle. Gilbert de Clare, Lord of Glamorgan built it on land claimed by Humphrey de Bohun, Lord of Breconshire. There were many horse- and cattle-stealing raids, and an actual battle was reputed to have taken place near here called Maes-y-faenor. Edward I had Morlais Castle partly destroyed to prevent its use as a fortress.

◄ **MERTHYR TYDFIL**
Caedraw c1965
M118073

This photograph was taken from the cinder tips on the Rhydycar side of the River Taff; to the right are the Taff Vale railway buildings, which were converted to the road transport depot, and are now the site of a supermarket and bingo hall. The parish church is at the centre, and the newly built Caedraw School is on its left. Caedraw, an area of early housing, was redeveloped in the sixties.

► **MERTHYR TYDFIL**
The Parish Church c1965 M118076

The town originally grew up around the burial place of the Celtic Saint Tydfil. The old parish church of St Tydfil was restored and re-built in the 1890s; its graveyard was greatly reduced in 1902 to construct the road to Cardiff. Now a chapel of ease, the church survived an attempt to pull it down in the 1970s with the support of the poet John Betjeman.

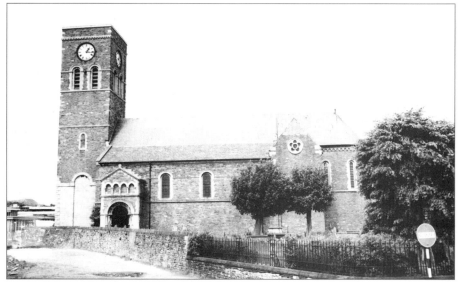

MERTHYR TYDFIL
High Street c1965
M118080

The vehicle on the right-hand side is a dark blue Merthyr Tydfil Corporation ambulance. The ornate building on the right was then the New Inn; it subsequently became a Burger King, and is now a McDonalds. The two clothing shops, Masters & Co and Weston's (left), have been replaced by other businesses. The policeman standing on the road (left) was then part of the former Merthyr Tydfil County Borough Police Force.

MERTHYR TYDFIL
High Street c1965
M118081

The jeweller's shop, H Samuel (centre distance), which was beneath the clock, was once the former Post Office. Samuel's Corner had a certain reputation in Merthyr Tydfil. The Arcade Café (right) was run by Italians and specialised in home cooked pasta. On the left beyond Bevans and Halfords was Rosie Royal's; she ran a greengrocer's and a wet fish shop, and everyone knew her. Hanging from the King's Arms is a Hancock Brewery sign (right).

◄**MERTHYR TYDFIL**
*Taff Fechan Valley
and Pontsticill c1965*
M118102

This rural valley, in the
parish of Vaynor, was in
Breconshire until 1974.
Pontsticill is an old
community, and in recent
years it has undergone
many changes. The
Baptist chapel has been
converted into a
residential dwelling. Two
public houses here, the
Red Cow and the Butchers
Arms, have a long history.

◀ **MERTHYR TYDFIL**
Hoover Ltd c1965
M118086

Opened in 1948, the Hoover factory was built near the site of the Plymouth Ironworks. This factory was built to manufacture the Hoover electric washing machine and was, until recently, the main employer in the area. The housing forming a triangular shape on the left was a unique example of early industrial dwellings, but it was demolished, despite protests, in December 1977.

◀ **MERTHYR TYDFIL**
The Taff Fechan Reservoir c1965 M118107

Despite the heavy rainfall, the supply of clean drinking water was once a problem in Merthyr Tydfil. One medical officer of health described the water as being scant and 'disgustingly foul'. The early reservoirs were becoming inadequate by the turn of the century, and in 1911 an Act of Parliament was obtained to impound the waters of the Taff Fechan by constructing a dam at Pontsticill. The Taff Fechan Reservoir, completed in 1927, has a capacity of 3,400 million gallons, and a length of over 2 miles. Water is supplied to Aberdare, Merthyr Tydfil and Rhymney.

RHYMNEY, *From the Station c1955* R270005

The stretch of buildings on the other side of the station were once the original
Company Shop (of the Rhymney Iron Company), which was set up and strictly
run by Andrew Buchan - there was another similar shop towards the upper end
of Rhymney. The buildings still exist, but are now used for a different purpose.
This picture gives a fine view up Surgery Hill and across the middle of Rhymney.

RHYMNEY, *The Memorial c1955* R270011

The Rhymney war memorial to commemorate the local men who gave
their lives in the Great War was erected in 1929 and unveiled in the
October of that year. Obviously, the names of the soldiers of the Second
World War, which are also on the monument, were added to the plinth
much later.

▼ **RHYMNEY,** *The Park, the Bowling Green c1955* R270013

The park, correctly known as the Rhymney Memorial Park, was founded and opened in 1925 by the Rhymney Town Council. The figures on the bowling green reveal that this facility was well used, despite its exposed position.

► **RHYMNEY**
Bute Town c1955
R270015

Bute Town (Drenewydd), on the top left-hand side, was modelled after a rural Cumbrian village. Middle right (just off the picture) was the site of the Union Iron Works, the first in the area, built in 1802 at the Garn. The remnants of this furnace can still be seen today, and the manager's house is still in existence as a modern hotel.

◄ **RHYMNEY**
The River c1955
R270017

The Rhymney river was the meeting place of three South Wales counties, Breconshire, Glamorgan and Monmouthshire, and also the boundaries of the great estates of Bute, Beaufort and Morgan. The old traditions of 'beating' and 'walking' the boundaries survived here longer than most places because of their great significance.

► **RHYMNEY**
Carno Bridge
c1955 R270018

In its earliest days the Carno ford was used for the conveyance, by mule and pack horse, of iron ore to the Dowlais Iron Works from the Ras Bryn iron mines. At 1093 feet above sea level, this area was one of the earliest industrial communities in Rhymney, although it is hard to imagine that now.

RHYMNEY
High Street 1967
R270031

On the left, the library has become the health centre, and the ex-servicemen's club is closed, but Lloyds Bank is still open. The Workmen's Club is still on the right, but Carline the jeweller has moved to Merthyr Tydfil. There is no longer a post office next to the ornate and elegant Scala Cinema (second from the right), and the Rhymney General Stores (extreme right) is now a chemist's.

► **TREDEGAR**
*The Town Clock and
the Circle c1955*
T265007

This view from the top of
Morgan Street shows the
72ft-high ornamental
clock tower and three of
the four roads that lead
from the Circle. The
tower's iron steps were
enclosed with iron
railings until 1933, when
the present dwarf wall,
pillars and sward were
substituted. The date of
1858 on the base of the
clock is misleading, as it
was not completed until
1859. The Olympia
cinema and the Black
Prince public house are
on the left, and situated
just to the right of the
clock is the Tredegar
Arms, commonly
known as the TA. The
impressive mock-Tudor
building behind the
clock is no longer the
electricity department.

◄**TREDEGAR**
*The Council Offices
c1955* T265010

These council offices, set
in Bedwellty Park, were
once a private mansion
known as Bedwellty
House, built for the
Ironmaster Samuel
Homfrey. At the
beginning of the 20th
century there was a large
fountain in front of the
house. There were glass-
houses to the left, and
around the back of the
house there was a huge
ice-house.

▲ **TREDEGAR,** *Bedwellty Park c1955* T265019

The bandstand in Bedwellty Park was presented to the town by the Tredegar Athletic Club. The elegant roof on the bandstand has now been replaced by a plainer triangular one. The gardens here are in the ornamental Chinese style. The ladies' shelter in the park was well known to courting couples, but unfortunately this building became so vandalised that it has now been demolished.

◄ **TREDEGAR**
The Largest Block of Coal c1955 T265030

This huge lump of coal, weighing about 15 tons, was cut by Mr John Jones, an employee of the Tredegar Iron & Coal Co. It was a great feat to extract such a weight. The coal was intended to be sent to the Great Exhibition in Crystal Palace, 1851, but it was too heavy to move. There is now a roof over the coal and a pit cage alongside.

TREDEGAR
General View c1955
T265034

The impressive building towards the middle of the picture was Penuel, a largely Welsh-speaking chapel; a nursing home is now on this site. Saron chapel stands alongside Market Street on the extreme right. The roof of the fire station can be seen in the foreground. The tips in the background have now all been landscaped, and the distant chimney belongs to the number Nine Colliery, which closed in the 1920s.

TREDEGAR, *Castle Street c1965* T265064

The town clock has been given a number of nicknames, including 'the Iron Duke of Tredegar', because of the small profile of the Duke of Wellington on the base. 'The Great Iron Clock of Tredegar' has been described as 'a misshapen lighthouse' and 'an outsized dumbbell', amongst other terms of endearment. As we look down Castle Street, we can see the NCB Club on the right. There used to be a Braces' Bakery near to the Glyn Café. The area had a large number of public houses: on the corner was the Cambrian Public, on the right-hand side was the Kings Head, on the left was the Golden Lion, and the Black Prince was just around the corner.

INDEX

NAMES OF SUBSCRIBERS

The following people have kindly supported this book by subscribing to copies before publication.

Mr R Adler, Merthyr Tydfil

The Atkinson Family, Rhymney & Bargoed

A G Baker

John B Baldwin, Merthyr Tydfil

Mr & Mrs L Ball, Ebbw Vale

The Bampfield Family, Tredegar

The Bann Family of Ebbw Vale

Alf Barlow & Janet Thomas, Rhymney

To Barrie, Christmas 2004 love Kay

Mr Dennis Baynham from Aberdare

Mr David Bevan, Cwmaman, Aberdare

Mrs Mavis Bosley

Glyn & Anne Bowen, Merthyr Tydfil

Jan Karl Bowen, Merthyr Tydfil

Kurt Mark Bowen

Brown & Gummett Families, Darrah/Deri

Mr I J Bull & Mrs N E Bull, Ebbw Vale

The Burns Family, Methyr Tydfil

Dennis C Butler, Merthyr Tydfil

The Bythell Family, Brynmawr

In memory of Mr & Mrs F C Cable, Brynmawr

In memory of Mr & Mrs R A Cable, Brynmawr

Tony Campbell, Brynmawr

Dai Carlyon, Aberdare

Edna Margaret Chidgey

Mr C & Mrs M Church, Ebbw Vale

In memory of our son, Kenneth John Clark

The Colcombe Family

In memory of Colin, Betty & Paul Cooper

Glyn, Doreen, Brian Collins, Merthyr Tydfil

For my Parents Bill & Vera Crompton

Cynon Valley Leader

Brandon D Davies, Merthyr Tydfil

Brian Colin Davies, Blackwood

Cicely Davies, Blaina

David Graham Davies, Tredegar

Des Davies, Ebbw Vale on his 64th birthday

The Davies Family of Bronhaul, Cwmbach

The Davies Family of Merthyr Tydfil

Eirwyn Davies, Trecynon, Aberdare

Ivor Davies, Merthyr Tydfil

Mr Keith Davies, Ebbw Vale

Miss L Davies, Mr R Price, Merthyr Tydfil

Mark Hilton Davies, Tredegar

Maureen Davies, Brynmawr

Mr & Mrs P Davies, Aberdare

Richard D Davies, Aberdare

To Thomas Davies

Mr W A Davies, Merthyr Tydfil

Mrs Wendy E Davies, Aberdare

Ray & Lyn Davis, Cwmaman, Aberdare

To Uncle Den love Luke, Todd & Holly

To Den & Kath love Luke, Todd & Holly

The Derrick Family, Aberdare

Charles Docton, Merthyr Tydfil

D S Dowling, Merthyr Tydfil & S A Dowling, Rhymney

To Raymond Doyle, Souvenir of Wales

The Edmunds Family, Foundry Town, Aberdar

Mrs Sydney Edwards-Jones

Alan Evans, Rhymney

David Evans, Ebbw Vale

Gareth T Evans & Valerie Evans, Cefn Coed

John Evans, Rugeley

Richard & Eileen Evans, Merthyr Tydfil

Terence Evans, Penywaun, Aberdare

In memory of David Farr, Brynmawr

John Farrington

Peter Firth, Canada; Mam, Merthyr Tydfil

As a tribute to my Parents Olwen & Bill Flaherty

Graham Foley, Beaufort

E Forrester, Aberdare

To Nancy Foster from the Star Girls, Merthyr

Mr K France, Aberdare

Happy Memories, Shirley G

Peter George

In memory of Glyn & Peg, Hirwaun

Mr Alan C Goodenough, Brynithel

R Gooding, Monmouth

Wilfred Gray

Harold P T Greaves, Ebbw Vale

To Jean & Ken Griffiths from Rosa & Colin

Gwent Gazette

Rev M Hagerty, Ebbw Vale

In memory of Liz & Bob Hall, Aberdare

Mr W E Hallam, Cwmfelinfach

Gerald & Betty Hargest, Tredegar

Roger & Janice Harriman, Ebbw Vale

The Harris Family, Ebbw Vale

Thomas S Hill & Anne M Hill, Dowlais

Mr R & Mrs M Hollmann, Ebbw Vale

Mr J & Mrs K Holly

The Hope Family, Galon Uchaf, Merthyr

To my Daughter Teigan Hope, Nov 04, Merthyr

Hugh Hopkins, Aberdare

Mr & Mrs David & Gwyneira Howells, Robertstown

Mr J E Howells, Rhymney

The Hughes Family, Rhymney

Brinley Humphreys, Aberdare

David Rhys Hungerford

The Hunt Family, Trelewis

B M James, L James, Aberdare

Mostyn J Isaac

Peter & Judy James and Family, Merthyr Tydfil

Mr & Mrs J Jeffs, Lowick

In memory of 'Bob' John, Ponlottyn

The Johnson Family, Merthyr Tydfil

Alan Wishlade Jones

To Alun Jones Christmas 2004, Cardiff

In memory of Betty Jones, Dowlais

Mr D L & Mrs R Jones, Aberdare

Gillian Jones

Mr Ivor Jones

Ron Jones, Merthyr Tydfil

In memory of Thomas A E Jones, Merthyr

In memory of Wulf B J Jones, Merthyr Vale

Mr & Mrs John & Lois Kehely

Mr Max & Mrs Judy King, NL, Canada

Mr & Mrs D Lake, Brynmawr

The Law family, Merthyr Tydfil

Mr R Lawrence, Aberdare

In memory of Marilyn Letch

Mr B & Mrs E E Lewis, Merthyr Tydfil

The Lewis Family, Cwm, Ebbw Vale

Hor Lewis

John & Ann Lewis, Thomastown

Iris & Ivor Lewis, Ebbw Vale, Christmas 04

Roy Lewis, Merthyr Tydfil

Thomas Lewis, Merthyr Tydfil

In memory of Michael Linehan, Merthyr

Diane A Lloyd, Tredegar

Lynda Lloyd & Family, Aberaman

Cyril & Ann Lock, Cwmbach, Aberdare

Herbert B Low

McAdams, 12 Mill Street, Aberdare

Ron & June Mabe, Trinant, Ebbw Valley

Ivor B C Mainwaring, 'A Cefn Coed Boy'

To Mansel, Merry Xmas love you, Margaret

Mr & Mrs Howard Mansell, Aberdare

Les & Sandra Martin, Pant, from Ann

Shawn Mercer, NL, Canada

Merthyr Express

Stephen John Milton

Mr V & K Moran & Family, Merthyr Tydfil

Ivor & Phyllis Morgan, Aberdare

Tim Morgan, Merthyr Tydfil

William Alcwyn Morgan, Merthyr Tydfil

In memory of D Morgans, Merthyr Tydfil

Albert George Morris

Marion Morris

William S Morris, Aberdare

Mr Colin Neagle, Merthyr Tydfil

In memory of Gwyn Newbury, Nantyglo

Bernard Nicholas, Merthyr Tydfil

Gran & Gramps Nicholas love Sam & Georgia

Christopher Nicholls, Merthyr Tydfil

In memory of Nancy Norbury, Merthyr

Bill Overbury with love Mavis & Vince

Ms Doreen Pardy, NL, Canada

Keith Parfitt, Abertillery

Kelvin Parfitt, Abertillery

Mr R K & Mrs I Parry

Ronald Vivian Parsons, Six Bells, Abertillery

Gary Perrin, Rhymney

To Pete Love from Babs

Mr & Mrs Phillips, Hobby Horse, Brynmawr

R J Phillips, Merthyr Tydfil

The Powell Family, Ebbw Vale
Julia Price-Abbott & Gareth Abbott of Aberdare
James Price, Pontlottyn
Ken Price, Merthyr Tydfil
Morgan & Tiegan Price of Merthyr Tydfil
Mr W A & Mrs M L Price, Gurnos, Merthyr
A Prince, Merthyr Tydfil
Miss Christine Rees
Dafydd & Margaret Rees, Frank Duffy
Raymond Rees
T Rees, Merthyr Tydfil
Rhymney Valley Express
To John F Richards from Philip & family
Stuart Richards
P C Bert Robins
Roy Sankey on his 88th birthday
Alyn Saunders, Talybont On Usk
Mr & Mrs C Scott, Aberdare
The Sellick Family, Mountain Ash
Harry Sherman, formerly of Merthyr
The Snow Family, Merthyr Tydfil
Angela Snowdon, Vic Coughtrey, Ebbw Vale
For my Father, Jeff Southcott
The Sparkes Family, Aberdare
The Star Family, Merthyr Tydfil
In memory of Selby Star, Methyr Tydfil
G Stevens, Ebbw Vale & L C E Evans, Aberdare
Danny Sullivan, Merthyr Tydfil
Brynley Sutton Esquire of Merthyr Tydfil
The Taylor Family, Merthyr Tydfil
Leanne Taylor, Aberdare
Bernard Thomas OBE, Quakers Yard
Elaine & Billy Thomas, Merthyr Tydfil
Garfield Thomas of Aberdare
Jane Thomas, Brynmawr
Jennett Iris Thomas
Maldwyn Glyndwr Thomas, Cwmbach

Philip Thomas, Aberdare
In memory of Trevor & Edith Thomas
Trevor Thomas, Merthyr Tydfil
Mr P & Mrs C Tidcombe, Aberdare
In memory of Dr R Topping, Tredegar
Jeff & Lynne Tucker, Ebbw Vale
D G Turley, Aberdare
Martyn Turner
Paul Turner
Dai Vaughan, Queens Rd, love Mary & kids
Fred & Ada Vaughan, Tredegar
To the Walsh Family, Bedford
Mr Richard L Walsh, Yew St, Troedyrhiw
Mr & Mrs A G Walton, Merthyr Tydfil
Mr & Mrs B Waters & Family, Brynmawr
The Webb Brothers of Llwydcoed, Aberdare
Maureen & John Webb, Newport
Jean Webster of Brynmawr
Denver Whale, William G Whale
W T White
Mr & Mrs M & A Wigley, Llwydcoed
Alan C Williams, Mountain Ash
Barbara & Rhydian Williams of Aberaman
Creighton H Williams, Ebbw Vale
Ireen Williams, Aberdare
John & Elizabeth Williams, Aberdare
John & Glenys Williams, School St. Tir-Phil
Kenneth & Edith Williams, Merthyr Tydfil
The Malcolm Williams Family, Godreaman
Melvin William Williams, Merthyr Tydfil
T E Williams, Aberdare
Doris Wilson, Aberdare
Mr & Mrs Gerald & Janet Wilson, Waunlwyd, Ebbw Vale
D E W C Woodman, S D Woodman & W M Woodman
John Eric James Woodward
The Wreglesworth and Bailey Families

FREE PRINT OF YOUR CHOICE

Mounted Print
Overall size 14 x 11 inches (355 x 280mm)

Choose any Frith photograph in this book.
Simply complete the Voucher opposite and return it with your remittance for £2.25 (to cover postage and handling) and we will print the photograph of your choice in SEPIA (size 11 x 8 inches) and supply it in a cream mount with a burgundy rule line (overall size 14 x 11 inches).
Please note: photographs with a reference number starting with a "Z" are not Frith photographs and cannot be supplied under this offer.
Offer valid for delivery to one UK address only.

PLUS: Order additional Mounted Prints at HALF PRICE - £7.49 each (normally £14.99)
If you would like to order more Frith prints from this book, possibly as gifts for friends and family, you can buy them at half price (with no additional postage and handling costs).

PLUS: Have your Mounted Prints framed
For an extra £14.95 per print you can have your mounted print(s) framed in an elegant polished wood and gilt moulding, overall size 16 x 13 inches (no additional postage and handling required).

IMPORTANT!

These special prices are only available if you use this form to order . You must use the ORIGINAL VOUCHER on this page (no copies permitted). We can only despatch to one UK address. This offer cannot be combined with any other offer.

Send completed Voucher form to:
The Francis Frith Collection, Frith's Barn, Teffont, Salisbury, Wiltshire SP3 5QP

CHOOSE A PHOTOGRAPH FROM THIS BOOK

Voucher for **FREE** and Reduced Price Frith Prints

Please do not photocopy this voucher. Only the original is valid, so please fill it in, cut it out and return it to us with your order.

Picture ref no	Page no	Qty	Mounted @ £7.49	Framed + £14.95	Total Cost £
		1	Free of charge*	£	£
			£7.49	£	£
			£7.49	£	£
			£7.49	£	£
			£7.49	£	£
			£7.49	£	£
Please allow 28 days for delivery. Offer available to one UK address only			* Post & handling		£2.25
			Total Order Cost		£

Title of this book . . . .

I enclose a cheque/postal order for £ . . . .
made payable to 'The Francis Frith Collection'

OR please debit my Mastercard / Visa / Maestro / Amex card, details below

Card Number

Issue No (Maestro only)   Valid from (Maestro)

Expires   Signature

Name Mr/Mrs/Ms . . . .
Address . . . .
. . . .
. . . .
. . . . Postcode . . . .
Daytime Tel No . . . .
Email . . . .

Valid to 31/12/07

Free Print – see overleaf

Would you like to find out more about Francis Frith?

We have recently recruited some entertaining speakers who are happy to visit local groups, clubs and societies to give an illustrated talk documenting Frith's travels and photographs. If you are a member of such a group and are interested in hosting a presentation, we would love to hear from you.

Our speakers bring with them a small selection of our local town and county books, together with sample prints. They are happy to take orders. A small proportion of the order value is donated to the group who have hosted the presentation. The talks are therefore an excellent way of fundraising for small groups and societies.

Can you help us with information about any of the Frith photographs in this book?

We are gradually compiling an historical record for each of the photographs in the Frith archive. It is always fascinating to find out the names of the people shown in the pictures, as well as insights into the shops, buildings and other features depicted.

If you recognize anyone in the photographs in this book, or if you have information not already included in the author's caption, do let us know. We would love to hear from you, and will try to publish it in future books or articles.

Our production team

Frith books are produced by a small dedicated team at offices in the converted Grade II listed 18th-century barn at Teffont near Salisbury, illustrated above. Most have worked with the Frith Collection for many years. All have in common one quality: they have a passion for the Frith Collection. The team is constantly expanding, but currently includes:

Paul Baron, Phillip Brennan, Jason Buck, John Buck, Ruth Butler, Heather Crisp, David Davies, Louis du Mont, Isobel Hall, Gareth Harris, Lucy Hart, Julian Hight, Peter Horne, James Kinnear, Karen Kinnear, Tina Leary, Stuart Login, David Marsh, Lesley-Ann Millard, Sue Molloy, Glenda Morgan, Wayne Morgan, Sarah Roberts, Kate Rotondetto, Dean Scource, Eliza Sackett, Terence Sackett, Sandra Sampson, Adrian Sanders, Sandra Sanger, Jan Scrivens, Julia Skinner, David Smith, Miles Smith, Lewis Taylor, Shelley Tolcher, Lorraine Tuck, Amanita Wainwright and Ricky Williams.